Venice Comes Clean

Poetry by
Victoria Garton

Watercolors by John Garton

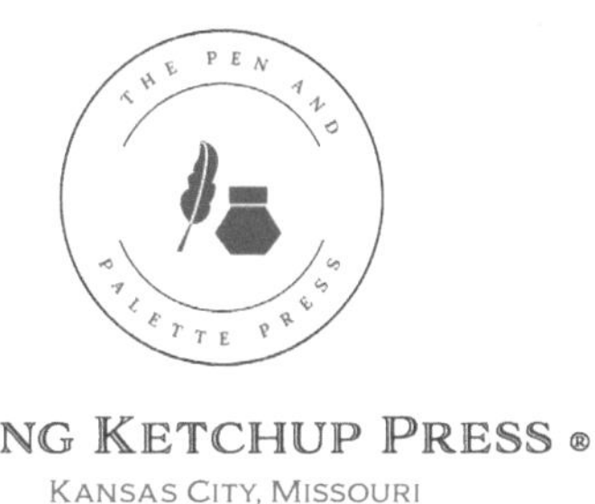

Flying Ketchup Press ®
Kansas City, Missouri

Grateful acknowledgment is made to the editors of the following publications where these poems first appeared: *Mid America Poetry Review*, "La Bibliteca at San Georgio Maggiore;" *Missouri Teachers Write*, "Coffeepot with Clinched Waist;" *The Same*, "Venice Comes Clean;" *Tower Poetry Society*, "A Tiny Kiss of Wax;" *Voices in Italian Americana*, "Along Lido's Fringe of Sandy Beaches," and "Some Indulgence."

......

All inquiries should be addressed to:

Flying Ketchup Press
11608 N. Charlotte Street,
Kansas City, MO 64115.

ISBN: 978-1-970151-80-0

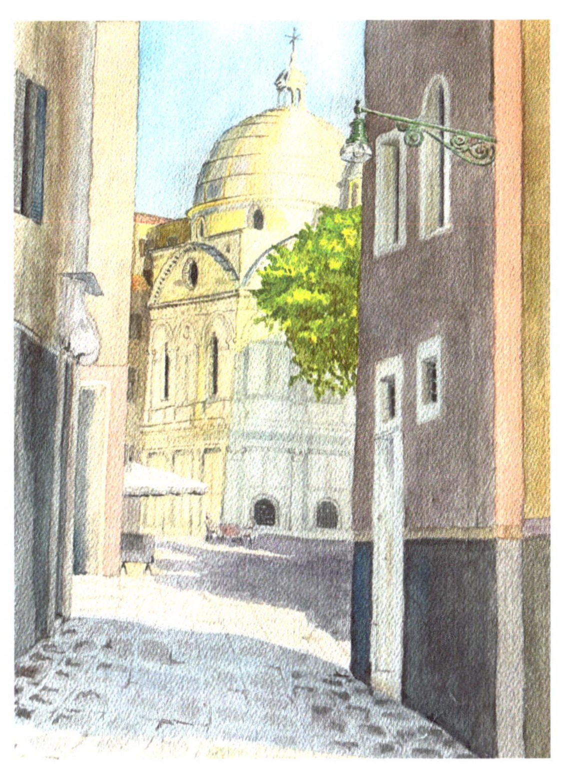

A Note from The Author

AS A MIDWESTERN GIRL, I dreamed of Venice, a place where roads were of water, not mud or gravel. So, when my son, John Garton, moved there to research and write his dissertation, I resolved to visit this place of antiquity and beauty. On breaks from teaching, I took a composition notebook and wrote my impressions in what became these poems. In Venice, I found a place where "we grow brighter than/our photos will record." It became possible "to double back/ from dead ends/ to find a way out/of life's mazes." Venice inspired my son to paint, and the book's watercolors will bring you also to "San Marco in the Rain."

~Victoria Garton

Contents

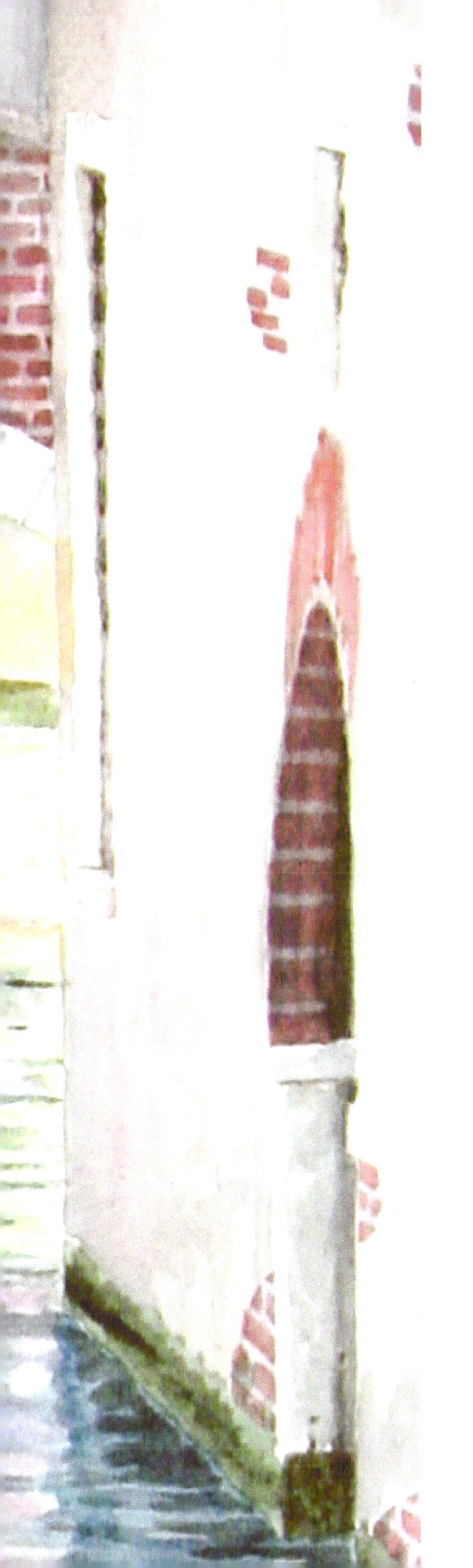

PART I

June 2002

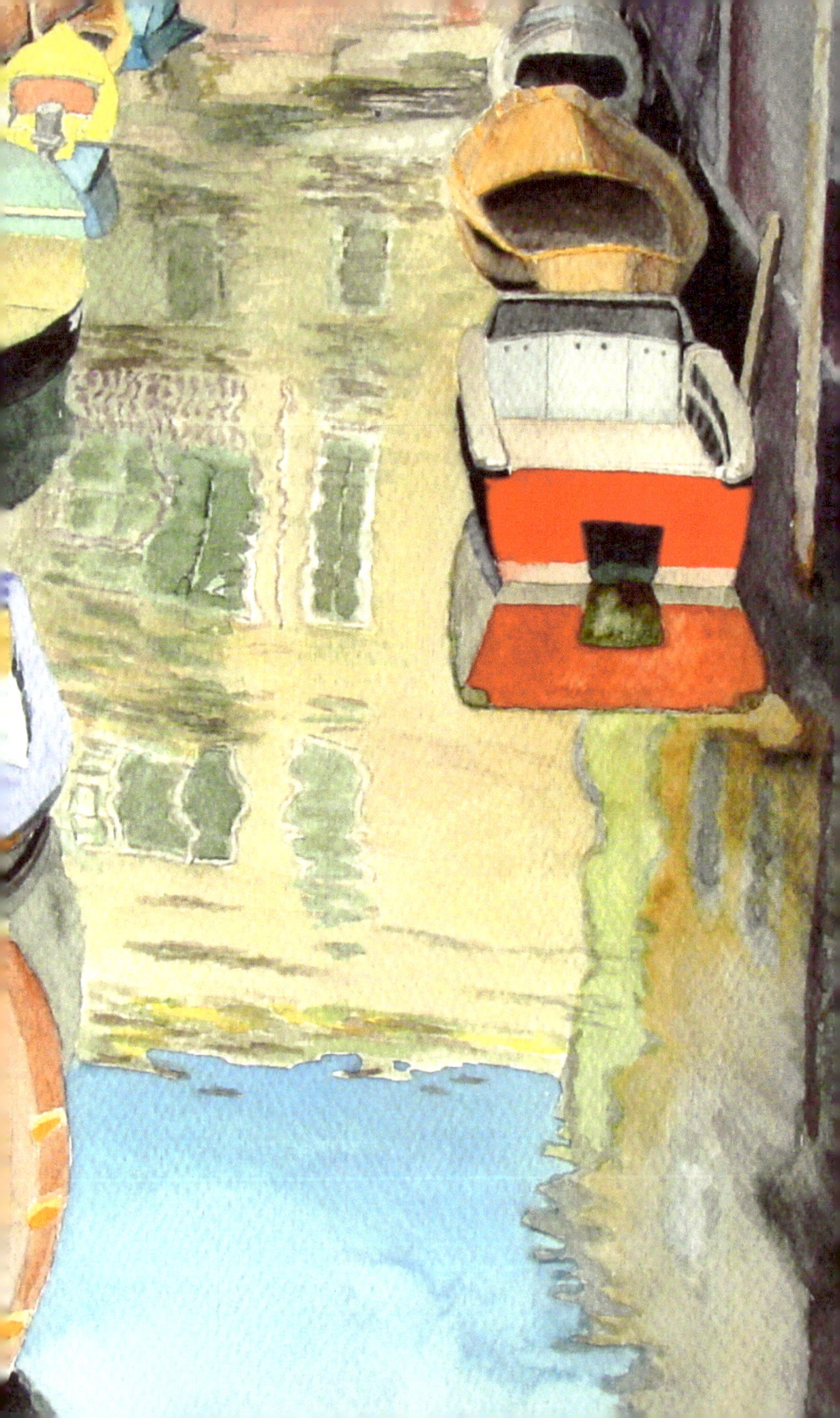

Sunny Apartment in Venice

for Maryfrances Cusumano June 27th

The sky through eight-foot
windows brightens this tiny
rented kitchen,
while just outside figs hang
above the courtyard
adding weight to their hips.

The tree opens broad green leaves
as I open a fellow poet's book.
Maryfrances has the greater claim
to Venice with Italian ancestors.
My family, English and Irish,
thought figs came under cellophane
in a skinny box at Christmas.

Still, I love to sit at this small
walnut table in our sunny apartment
reading of Uncle Phil and his fig trees
as if he were my uncle not hers.
Those trees tried to accommodate
Missouri winters like this chair
tries to accommodate full hips.

I write a postcard to Maryfrances
to say the trees of fruit still hold
to the dream of abundance
that propelled fathers and uncles,
Italian, Irish, and English
who left an old country for a new.

Coffeepot With Clinched Waist

Heavy as the gray receding night of rain,
it gathers heat like desires of youth
gather toward a boiling point. Years pass
and still passion rises like water in the pot
sucked through time's filter, through
the coffee's finest grind. Oh, the brew
up from fresh beans tastes of sweet rain.

Across the courtyard
gray plaster from centuries past
welcomes a Renaissance of sparrows.
They dip and weave a contentment
between longing and *joie de vivre.*
Maybe the sun will burst forth,
maybe not.

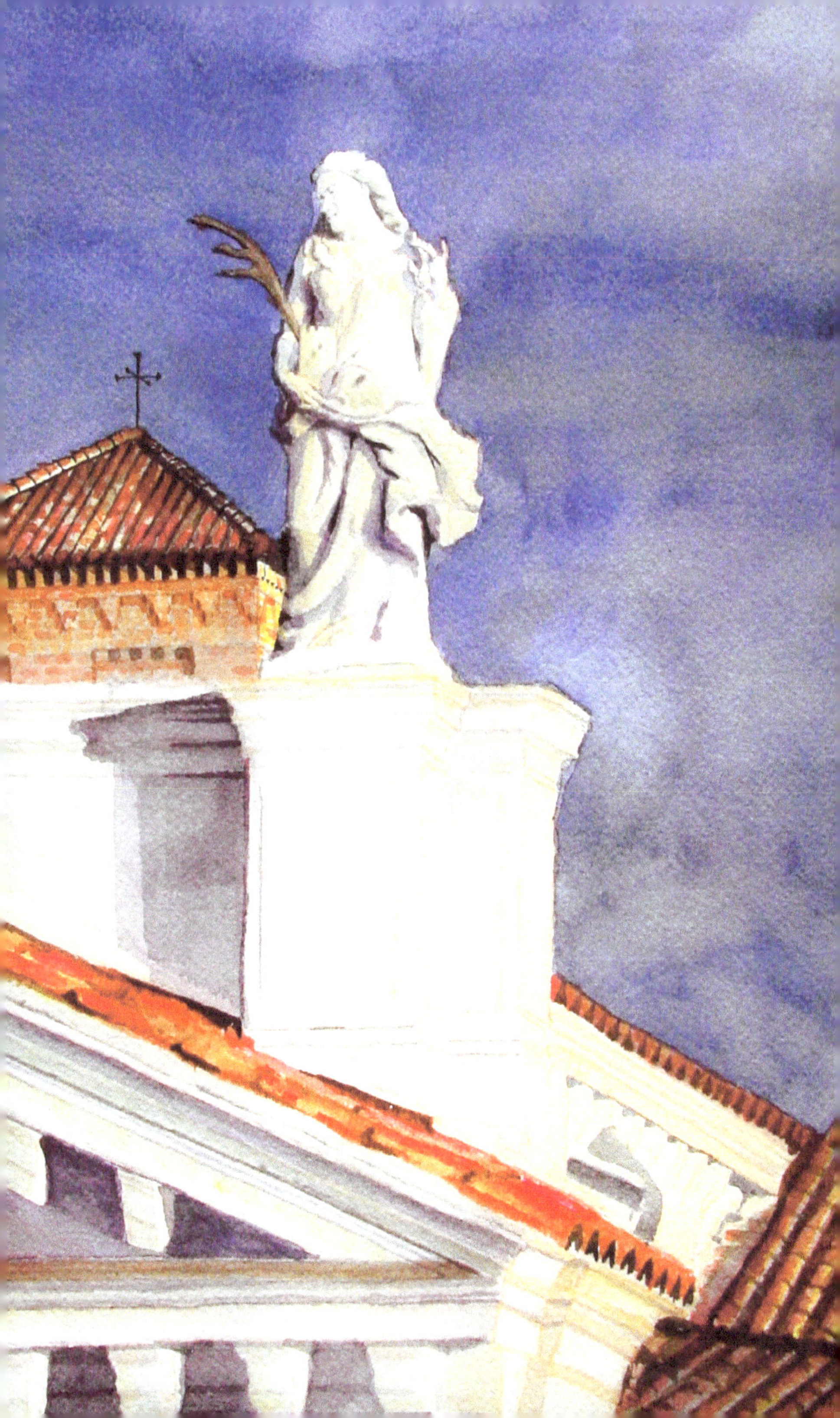

La Bibliotheca at San Giorgio Maggiore

If like a box this space should fold,
the wall from floor to ceiling
would lie half the length
of this long room. On the ceiling,
panels hold stories of the heart.

The scholar looks up to faces
sees spears, wings, and arms
uplifted to clouds, traces of which
billow still beyond high windows.
The mythical and divine look down,
over walnut-latticed cages,
to my son who knows each
by name and reputation.

Trying not to distract the scholar,
I bend over a blank page while
ghosts creak the high-backed chair.
I write this poem to Janus,
the only statue I recognize.
He looks both ways lest
the room fold upon itself.

A Tiny Kiss of Wax

My mother assumed the waxy look
of the dead a year ago.
Our son did not return to Missouri
but went to San Michele,
the cemetery island,
to give his grief to the dark cypress.

This spring as ground released
her daffodils to bloom again,
I scooped a vial of earth
that covered her and brought it
with my grief, but sentences I start
with her name get snuffed.

My husband and I come with our son
to *Santa Maria della Salute,*
built to celebrate deliverance
from the plague, to light
a candle for mother
in this solemn Baroque church.

Our prayers give way to laughter
as he tells of coming in November
with crowds from the city
and paying an altar boy to light,
puff, and rush to resell his candle,
a tiny kiss of wax on its wick.

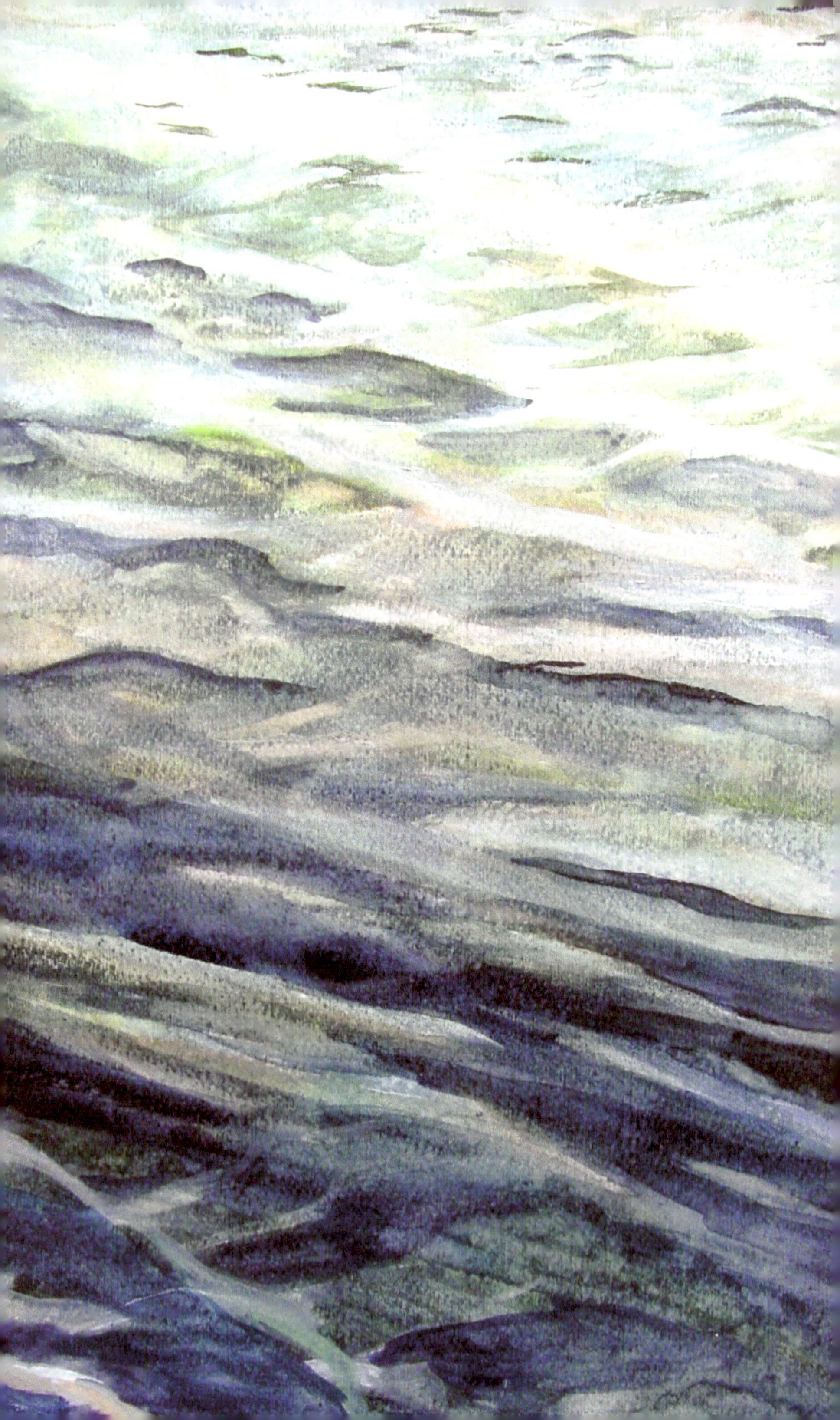

Some Indulgence

Some indulgence
allows the waves
to mesmerize
until the clouds
peak and break
in the same rhythms.

Some lenience
clears the way
for bells to ring
from towers
above the buildings
shoulder to shoulder.

This excess
stirs the quiet canals,
drops them so boats rise
called to that grand
serpentine from where
they will putter out,
to ride waves
on the Adriatic.

On the rhythm
of clouds and waves
and undulating bells,
the people
of Venice move
through centuries.

Il Gatto, the Cat

A cat bites the neck of its kitten,
claims like the papa kisses the neck
of the small boy who cannot be bothered,
who caresses his golden seine, holds fast
his green bucket. He will carry innocence
onto Lido's beach, chase gulls and surf
until love or duty calls him to bury
his adoring father in sand.

We call our cat *Il Gatto*–The Cat–and
will leave it behind just as we left
the cats of Rome to haunt the ruins.
This is our Venice cat. Someone
unseen fills its pan, strokes away fears,
keeps it friendly so it keeps to ankles,
meandering near as if coming along,
then padding forth at our late return.

Too shy to bite his neck or carry him along,
we follow our adult son to the beach.
Once he had a green bucket we filled
with love. His childhood haunts the ruins
of our collective past. We meander from it
and do not speak of love though it hangs
around like cats in the barn at home.
This love we take for granted until it
comes to us as *Il Gatto* in Venice.

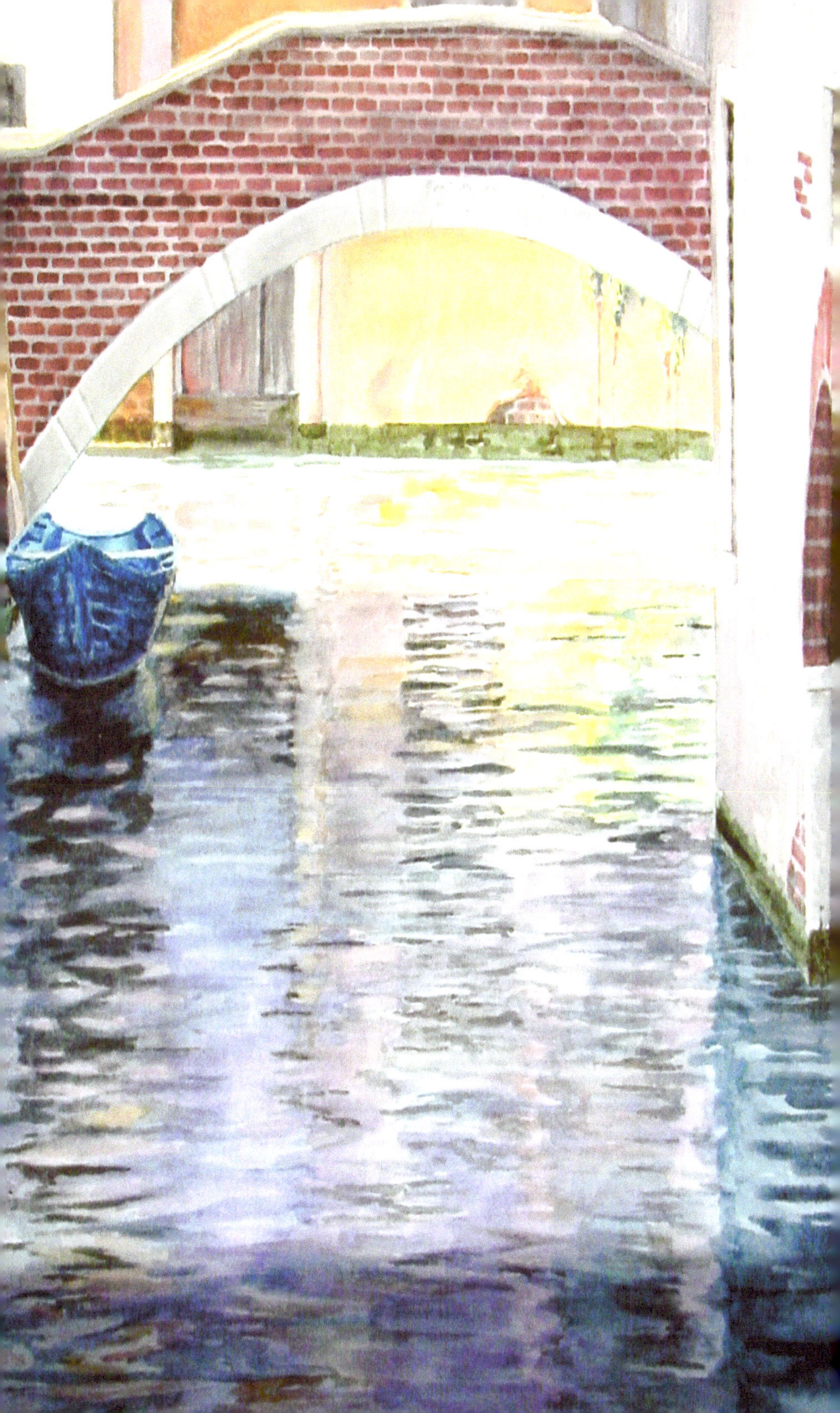

Along Lido's Fringe of Sandy Beaches

Sun toasts natives to deeper shades:
terra cotta, olive wood, chestnut,
and liver. We flash whiteness,
greased with sun block against pink,
scarlet, crimson, and flame.

The green Adriatic does not love
our Christmas colors. It calls
instead to brown sun worshippers
to lie on creamy rocks and bake.

We note the exposed breasts,
the mounded hips of those lying
in soporific idleness, marking
that length of fringe between
birth and death.

We note and pass on bicycles
not looking back. We work
our muscles as if life were
the urgent dip and lift of wind
along the spine of a strip of sand.

Was I Bewitched?

Attracted irresistibly to slender sandbank,
pointing a witch's finger,
dividing Venice and lagoon from Adriatic,
our son rides easy through festive streets,
calls out, "No one forgets how to pedal."
My husband on rented bike proves this true.

Meanwhile, doomed by dark spells
of narrowing shoulder
and fear of being splattered on the grill
of huge Iveco truck,
I wobble along with nerves jangling
brash as my bike's bell.

We ride for miles as the sea enchants
and calls us to sooth muscles,
swim out, in love with this day,
this life, the sea's salty kiss.
Charmed by clouds
we ride to the island's lower end.

Eat grilled cheese, take the ferry
to *Pellestrina,* bike on as if on magic brooms,
as if transformed by myth of agile youth.
We return under grilling sun
with hamstrings harping on
the long stretch as skin burns.

Off the bike, I follow
the mincing steps of a woman
in witch's pointy shoes.
Her toes are long as the isle of Lido.
We go as if circling a cauldron
while the sidewalk dips and rears.

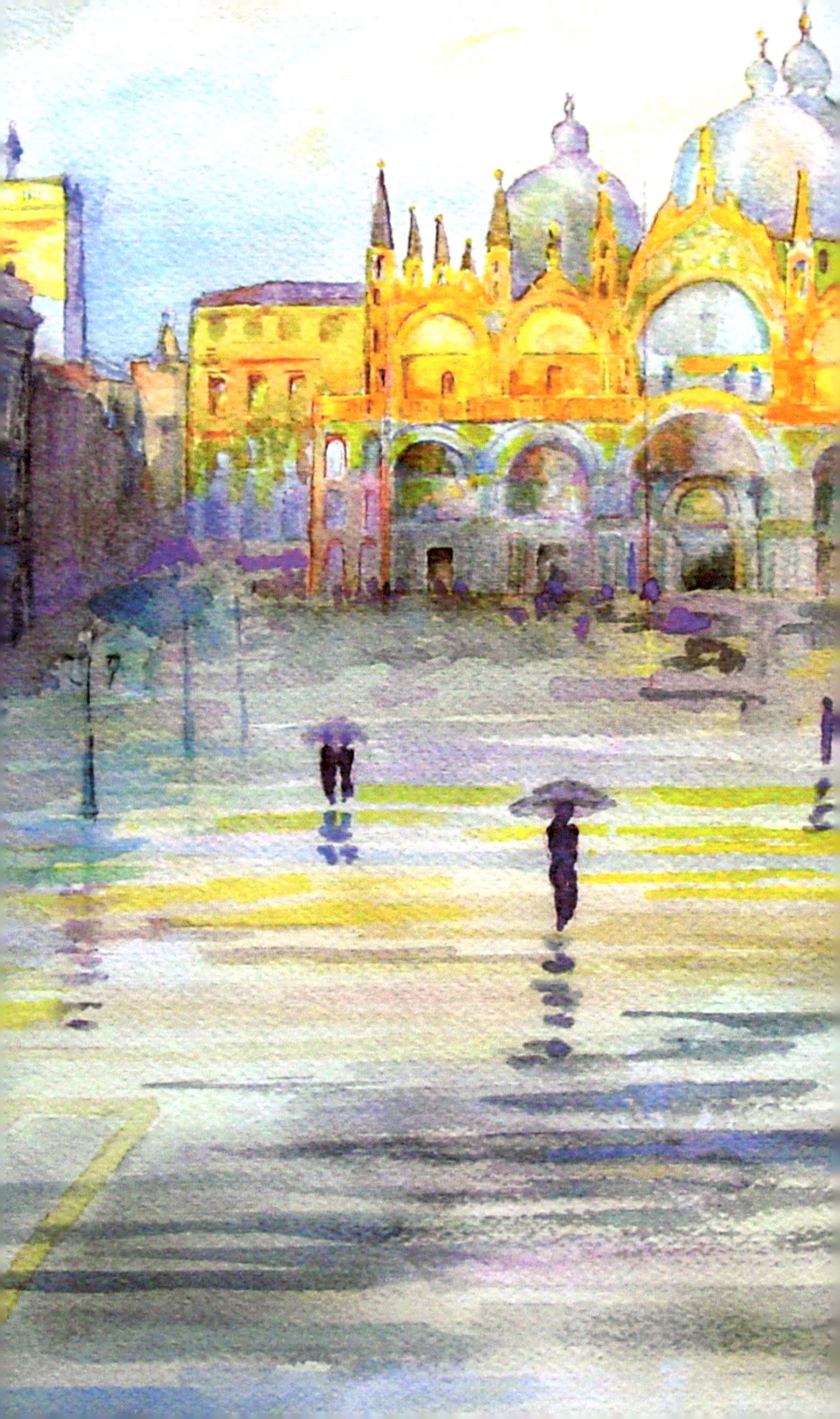

Venice Comes Clean

Like an errant Doge
the sun slips from the city
just before rain comes in torrents.
Water gushes where
ancient storm drains fail
filling alleys. It comes
under windowsills
to pool on floors near art.
Even the horses
on Basilica San Marco
blur in rain washing and
rinsing the dingy piazza.

Next day the sun returns
to bake its usual recipe
of tourists, but tile, stucco, and
stone have given up their heat.
On a clean horizon,
the towers and domes hang
like bleached laundry against
a sky where bluing spilled.

The stained past fades,
both ours and the city's.
In this Byzantine basin
we grow brighter than
our memories will allow.

On the *vaporetto* to *Torcello*
cool air raises goosebumps.
Attila the Hun's damp throne
chills to bone. Inside the cathedral
on a wall of Doomsday Mosaics
anguished faces rise from flames.
How they wish to stand bare headed
in a torrent like fell yesterday
cleansing the soul of Venice.

Burano at Noon

Psychedelic sunflower,
gas-flame blue,
phosphorescent green,
sunspot red:
the tablecloths
at *Ristorante Principe*
copy Andy Warhol's
polychrome glare
on a woman's face.

In the archipelago
this island's houses
wear the brightest colors.
If I had a pre-life,
I happily spent it here
and Andy lived next door
in a box of crayons.

Writing Good-bye on the Lagoon

Eyes of upper windows
sparkle with sun.
Water up to her knees,
Venice stirs her people
from dreams of drowning.
They fill cast-iron pots
and gaze out at roof tops
as the inferno builds
and water rises
through coffee grounds.

On the lagoon our *vaporetto,*
first of the morning,
writes *addio*. We board,
join travelers with duffels,
a few laborers with lunch-bags.

Postmen toss the mail from barge
to shore. A fish-seller poles
his rainbow of fins and fillets
past barges stacked with bottles
of water, enough to quench
the lovesick thirst of Venice.

Deadbolts click like teeth
behind the backs of lovers.
Il Gatto watches all, yet
turns an indifferent glance
as suitcases roll over stones
echoing *addio, addio.*

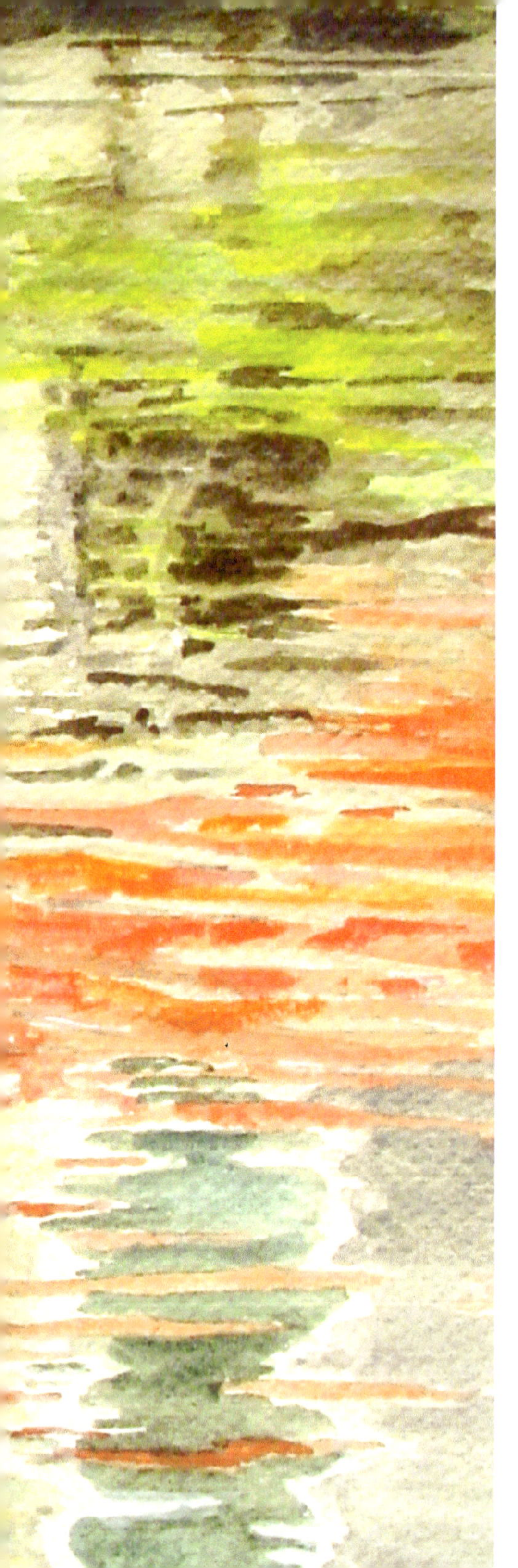

Part II

March 2003

Again to Venice

Again we come
to Venice
for the graceful
serpentines of water
instead of concrete,
brick, or macadam.
The substantial
holds in every other city.

Again we come
to Venice
to double back
from dead ends,
to find a way out
of life's mazes,
to fill the mind's canals,
to walk shaded alleys
to an unexpected bridge
and a piazza
where the sun
sits as light as froth
on cappuccino.

Again we come
to Venice
because life is more
than solid ground,
America's vast continent,
miles of interstate,
determined destinations
so we never lose our way.

Again we come
to Venice
to visit a son,
to sip bellinis abuzz
as bees at peach blossoms,
while mosquitoes nibble
ankles and waves
nibble foundations that
miraculously hold.

Murano on Monday

A leafy fern angles
from steps to canal.
It points whichever
way the waves go
following wakes
of small boats.
A March sun warms
mid-day.

A glassblower
works his iron rod
and lungs and from
a molten blob
a bird appears
ready to fly
out the door
as souvenir.

At noon working men
from furnaces fold
ham on buns, saw off
bites of cheese.
I eat this way at school,
work´s demands
put aside, my full
attention on food.

Sun in the Campo di Ghetto Nuovo

Where my husband and I sit in *Campo*
di Getto Nuovo, sun blesses plastic chairs,
paving stones, a bare trellis,
terra cotta pots with new growth,
an old woman in fedora smoking and warming,
the abandoned stone well,
a gray-green fountain threading its stream
to the drain, the cook coming from the canal
with boxes of ravioli, the green bottles
empty of *acqua minerale,* and the children
exuberant in flight playing a game of chase
as we all await the tour and stories
of 1516 when the Jewish population
were forced to live here and their children
were not so lucky, not so free,
but once so alive playing games that children
for centuries have played.

A Chance to Laugh

Had we not been looking
we might have missed
the camel in bas relief and
three silk merchants
leaning from niches
in *Campo dei Mori.*
Natives and tourists hurry
past these brothers
recessed into oblivion,
but *Signor Antonio Rioba,*
head hidden by turban,
has a metal nose too large
for his face.
Sometime since 1112
someone unskilled but well meaning
did rhinoplasty on *Signor Rioba.*
We laugh in spite of our
politically correct intentions
even as the face, stone still,
holds a quiet dignity.

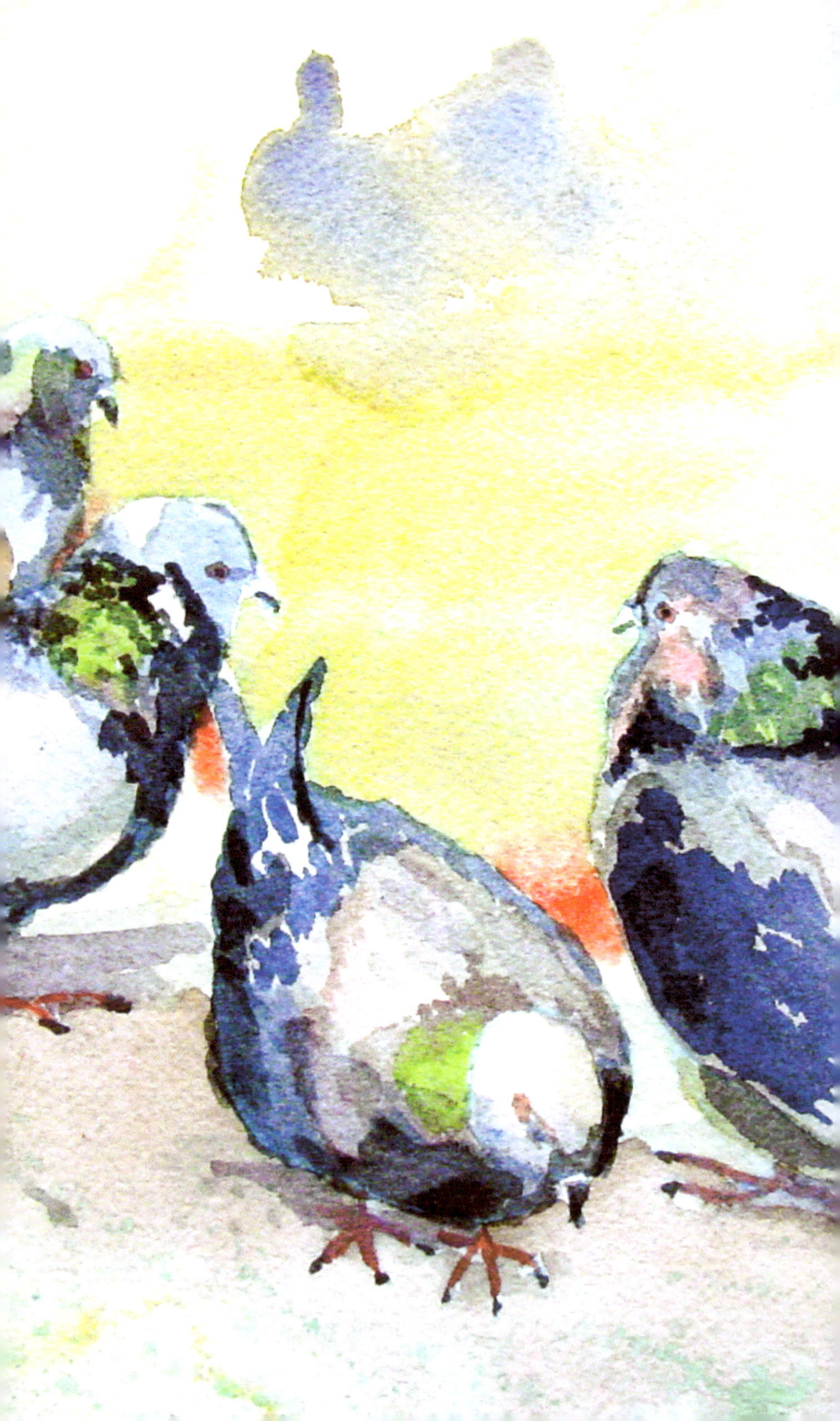

Pigeons of St. Marks

Pigeons carpet the piazza.
"Don't buy those pellets of pollution."
I shut my bag against hidden bread.
There is much to know about pigeons,
acidic shit, and monuments.

I had only wanted to hold bread in hands
and let arms branch.
Like Daphne turned to laurel tree,
I would give pigeons a place to roost
and pigeons would hide me from Apollo.

"Watch where you walk." I step from myth
to find excrement on my soles. Across the stones,
pigeons pad like monks to worship.
Each wears a hood and bows prayerfully.
"Wipe your feet as we enter the church."

The Doge's Palace

Where the Power Lay

So lifelike, Paolo Veronese's Saint Sebastian
could step from painted alcove except the saint
caught arrows, near an arm pit, near the groin.
He won't come from 1582 to warn of secret doors,
mezzanines, or attic places where power awaited
allegations slipped through the lion's mouth.

Saint Sebastian need not enter the room of the rope
to know the threat to shoulders forced so far back
ball and socket disjointed as the truth came out.
Power and politics pass away. Art endures, if time's
erasures don't clean the slate and ossified wood holds
and Saint Sebastian's wounds continue to bleed.

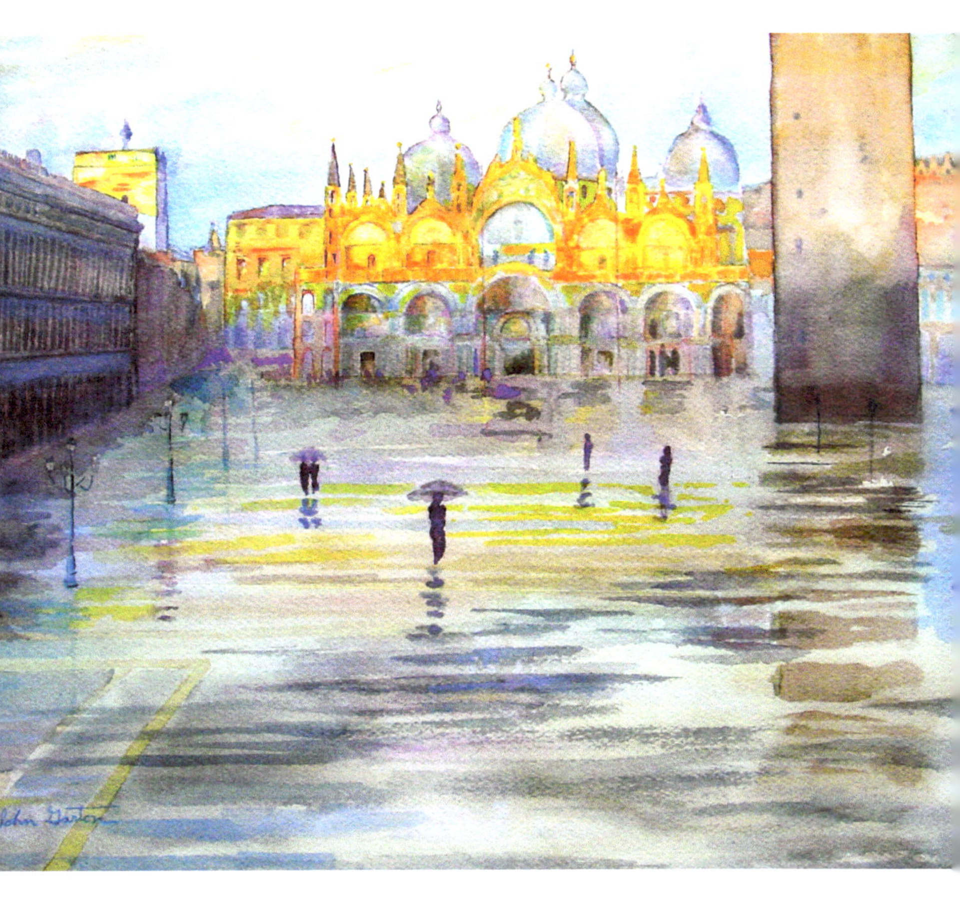

San Marco in the Rain
Watercolor on Paper

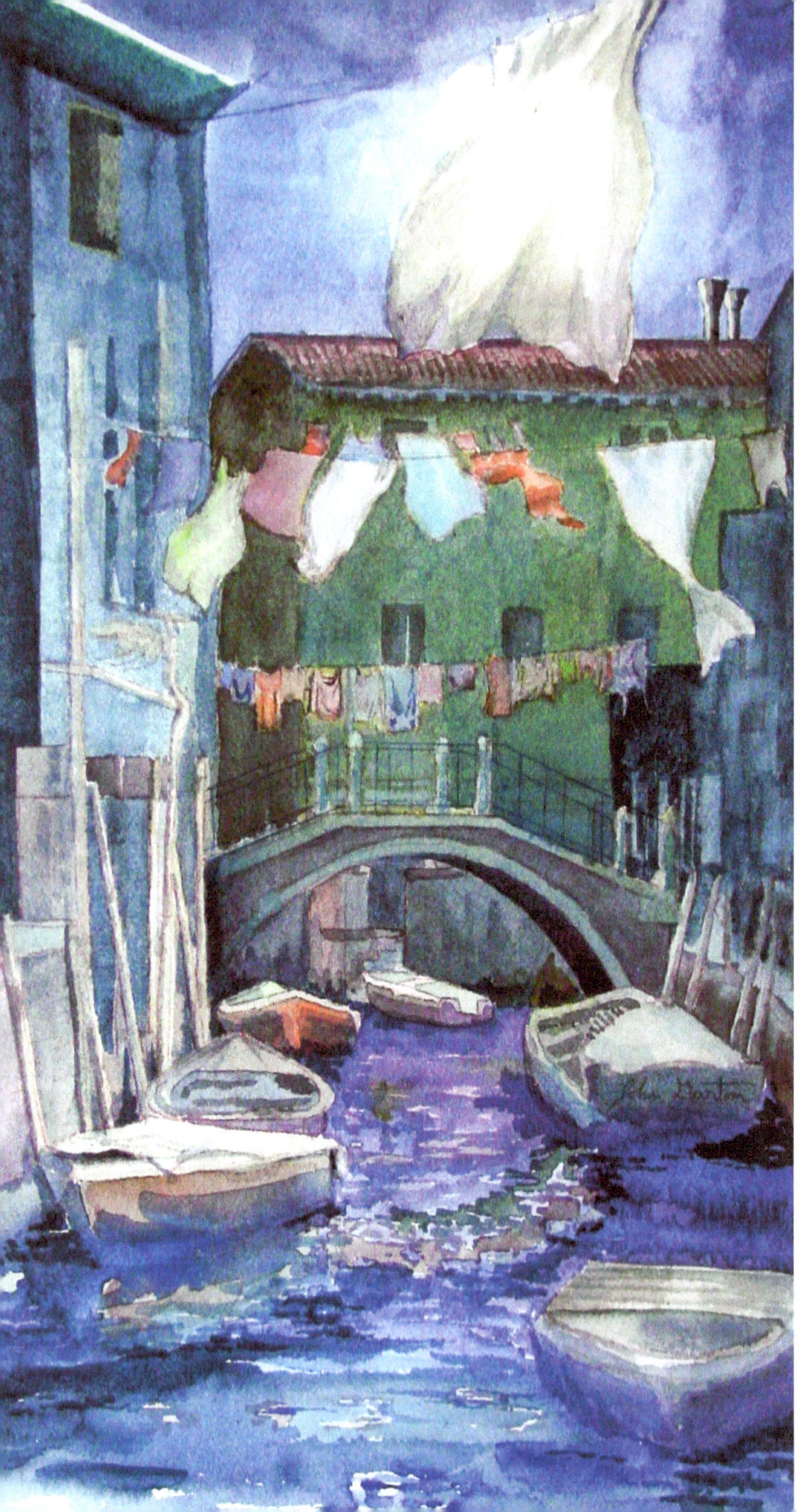

Night Laundry Overhead

March 15, 2003

Like darkened peace flags they flutter
through the night, fill as wind swirls
around the alleys. Ghost shapes remember
swell of thigh, chest heaving to take in breath.
Sometimes these second skins we drop
cling to stray hairs, flakes of shed skin
as if to keep some part of us as the evening
drops a curtain over St. Michele.

Without substance or wind our shadow selves
hang wet and limp. But on a windy night
these clothes flaunt their independence.
Kicking an empty leg, waving a handless arm,
they pantomime our fears like Mr. Bones.

This spring they wave beside banners
opposing our war. This we also fear, war
on spin cycle pulling in lives, spitting out
crumpled shirts. Highest above is a white sheet,
a glowing field to enshroud the moon.
Finding our way across the dim courtyard,
our spirits snap and beat to the violent wind
like this lonely linen restless for body and bone.

The Unvisited Dead

Cypress of San Michele
stand sentinel as daylight
abandons the battlefield
of waves and dusk folds
white caps in shadow.

Surrounded by lagoon,
the vanquished dead
stay under stones
as do the victors
and ordinary Venetians.

We will not visit
cypress, stones, or grief.
Terracotta walls stand high,
their great doors
locked.

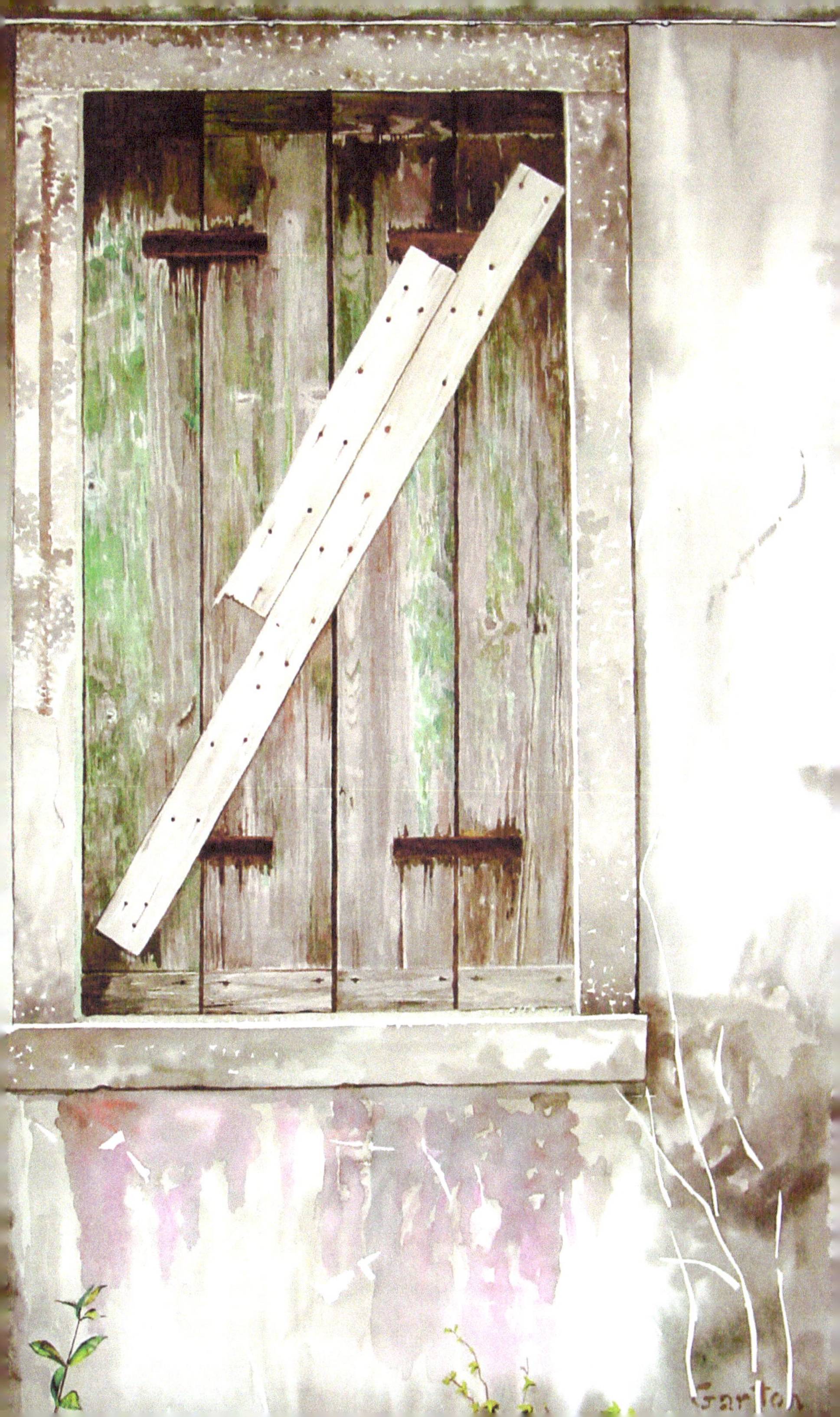
Garton

Delivering the Dissertation

Our son cradles the ream of paper
carefully bundled for travel. Behind him,
his father and I in victorious procession.
Down narrow alleyways, jubilant paving
stones resound to the Fed Ex Office.

From ideas gestated to words,
from research growing for two years,
(Every reference footnoted in painstaking
detail) he has written about portraits
painted by Paolo Veronese, a name
we struggle to pronounce.

We joke that it must not fall in water,
the airplane to New York must not crash,
his committee must bestow on him Doctor
of Philosophy, not leave him in limbo.
He gives it over to be boxed and blessed
and sent on the afternoon boat.

At the *Gallerie dell'Accademia* before
Veronese's Feast in the House of Levi
we celebrate with a soldier who has been
at the wine, a dog eyeing a cat at Jesus' feet,
a disciple picking his teeth, and the wealthy
of Venice reveling under triumphal arches.

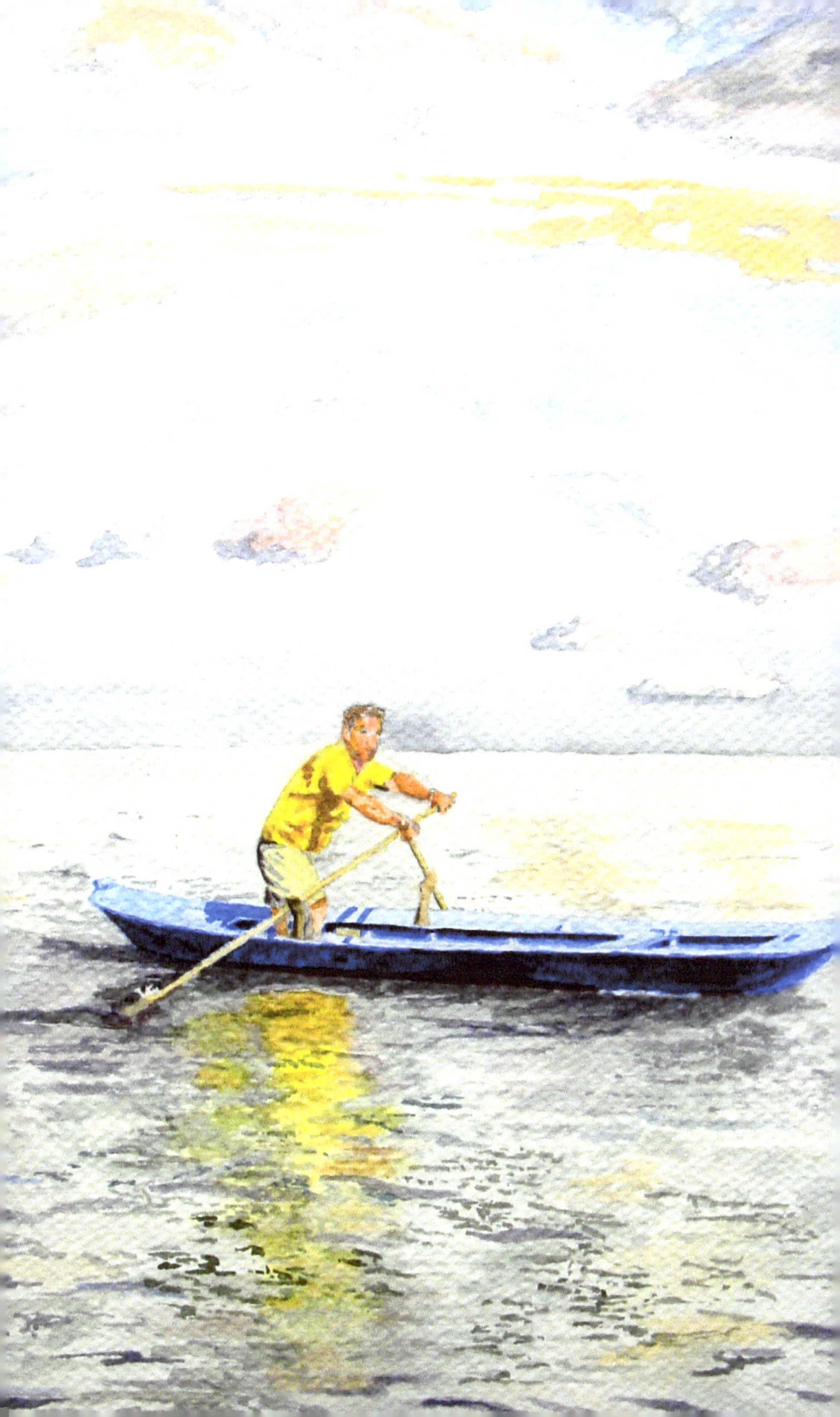

Seagulls Over Cannaregio

Gulls rise from the city's most northern *sestiere,*
leaving winded dogs barking on *terra firma.*
Giving wings to our longing, they deliver
to us the sky we knew before birth.
Hardly rowing at all, gulls turn and glide on
a cushion of air over the quays. They float
with grace, as we will, air giving way
as our jet turns to the homeward journey.

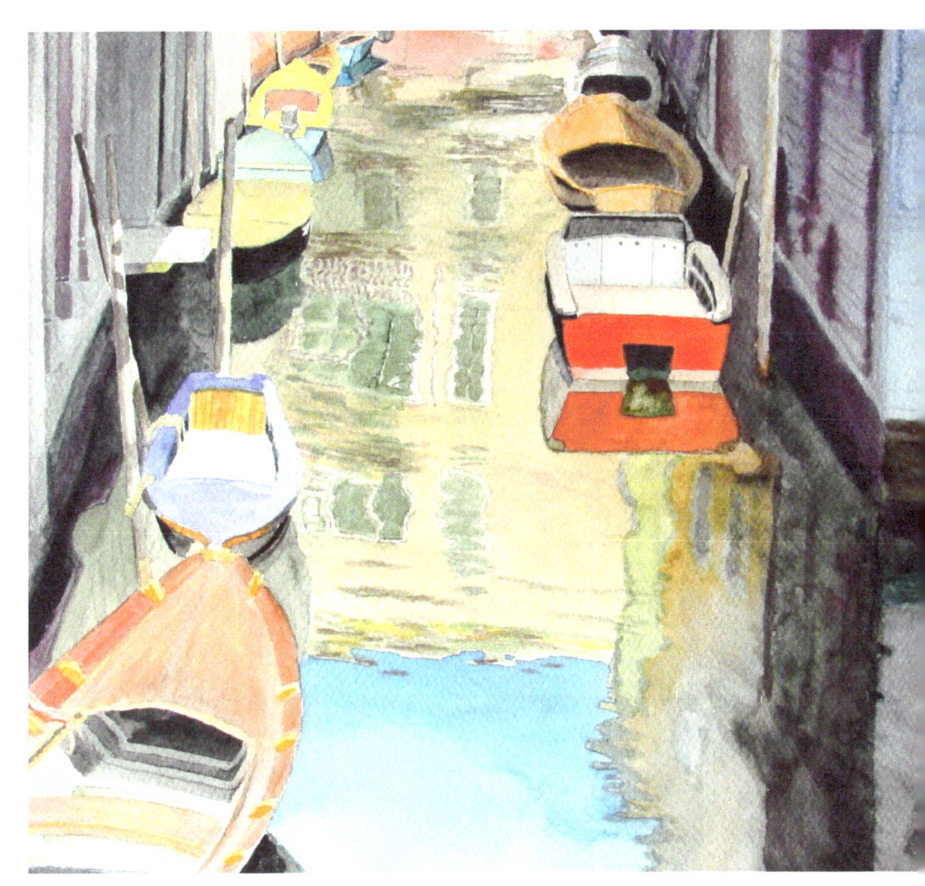

About the Author & Illustrator

VICTORIA GARTON came to poetry in a college classroom with poet Dave Smith in 1976. She was soon publishing in small magazines and journals such as: *Anima*, *Best Friends*, *High/Coo*, *Prairie Schooner*, *The Cape Rock*, and *The Spoon River Quarterly*. As a young mother, she taught and served on the Vernon County Commission. Garton found in poetry both an escape and a passion. Observing life, studying the work of poets she admired, delving for deeper meaning, and filling notebooks with first drafts were often done late at night after the chaos of daily life subsided. BkMk Press brought out her full-length collection, *Kisses in the Raw Night*, in 1989, and Finishing Line Press brought out a chapbook, *Pout of Tangerine Tango*, in 2022. A life-long educator, Garton taught for many years, the last fifteen teaching writing and literature for Crowder College. Married to a veterinarian and cattle producer, she has also published articles in *Working Ranch*, *Farm and Ranch Living*, and *Missouri Angus Trails*. She is the mother of two sons, George, a rancher, and John, an art historian and artist. Her two granddaughters, Irene and Edith, play the violin and dance.

JOHN GARTON, The poet's son, paints and lives in Central Massachusetts. He works in a variety of media. His paintings have been included in various juried exhibitions, including the Sprinkler Factory and ArtsWorcester in Massachusetts. In 2017, John was awarded a solo travel photography and video exhibition titled *On Roman Time* at Clark University. Dr. Garton is also an art historian specializing in Venetian Renaissance painting. He is the author of *Grace & Grandeur: the Portraiture of Paolo Veronese*, editor/co-author of *New Studies on Old Masters: Essays in Renaissance Art in Honour of Colin Eisler*, and articles on Titian, Leonardo da Vinci, and other artists. He is currently completing the book *The Sacro Bosco at Bomarzo: Landscape and Sculpture in Renaissance Lazio* (forthcoming with Brepols Publishers). His watercolors completed for this book of poetry were largely painted onsite while living in Venice, Italy.

www.ingramcontent.com/pod-product-compliance
Lightning Source LLC
LaVergne TN
LVHW052310100826
845147LV00006B/724

* 9 7 8 1 9 7 0 1 5 1 8 0 0 *